MW00931447

Priceless Parenting Guidebook:
Ideas for Handling Everyday Parenting Challenges

Kathy Slattengren, M. Ed.

Priceless Parenting® LLC
www.PricelessParenting.com
425-770-1629

Cover and Interior Design: Kathy Slattengren

Printed in the USA

Requests for such permission should be addressed to:

Priceless Parenting
15926 82nd Place NE
Kenmore, WA 98028

425-770-1629

www.PricelessParenting.com

Table of Contents

My Background

Parenting is the most important job we'll ever have. How we choose to parent our children will signficantly impact both our current and future happiness. Parents have told me they wish their children came with an owners manual to tell them how to handle the tough situations without breaking a sweat!

Unfortunately, babies don't come with manuals. However, there is a universal body of research and knowledge about how effective parents raise respectful, responsible children.

Through reading hundreds of parenting books, teaching numerous parenting classes and raising my own children, I have identified some of the best parenting practices. After parents learn and implement these best practices, they report having a lot more joy in their homes and a lot less yelling and nagging!

When I realized the tremendous impact this key parenting information had on families, I decided to make sharing this critical information my life's work. I wanted to ensure that all parents could learn these vital parenting skills at anytime, wherever they were located. To accomplish this I created online parenting classes combining my parenting knowledge with my degrees in instructional design, psychology and computer science.

Parents across the world have taken these online classes and enjoyed positive results in their relationships with their children. If you are interested in finding out more about the online class, you can try out the Setting Limits section for free at http://www.PricelessParenting.com.

You can also sign up to receive a free monthly newsletter which addresses common parenting challenges from yelling at kids when they misbehave to deciding on how much media is too much. Each newsletter focuses on one popular topic incorporating stories from real parents along with suggestions for applying the information to your own family.

The ideas described in this book are the same ones my husband and I used to raise our two children. Now that they are both teens, we are reaping the rewards of having responsible, considerate teens who are also a lot of fun. Please feel free to contact me if you have questions or would like to schedule a presentation or phone consultation.

I wish you all the best in your parenting!

Kathy Slattengren

Kathy.Slattengren@PricelessParenting.com
425-770-1629

This book will guide you through exploring new parenting ideas and trying them out with your own children.

This is your book:

- Write answers to the questions.

- Jot down your ideas.

- Record what works best for each of your children.

- Experiment with changing your behavior and write down what happens.

Plan to refer back to this book over the years as your children continue to grow and change.

Each age brings new challenges and insights!

Chapter 1: Guiding and Encouraging Children

We begin by examining key elements for building a positive family life. Each section has questions to help you think through how you can apply these ideas to your family.

Envisioning Our Ideal Home

Parenting is the most difficult job most of us will ever have. It is also an incredibly important job – the way we handle parenting will greatly affect our future happiness. This guidebook is designed to help you think through various parenting choices.

How we react to our children on a daily basis affects our relationship with them. By choosing approaches which include being compassionate and providing guidance, we will build warm, loving relationships with our children. In this chapter, we explore parenting behaviors that help build a strong foundation for understanding and guiding our children.

compassion + guidance = loving relationships

To begin with think back to the time when you were anticipating the arrival of your first child.

What were your dreams for this new family you were starting?

What type of home you did you hope to create?

I dreamed of creating a home that feels:

- **Welcoming**: Everyone in the family feels safe and secure. Home is a comfortable place to be and to share with friends.

- **Accepting**: Individuals are accepted for who they are and appreciated for their unique gifts, talents and contributions.

- **Supportive**: Family members help each other out.

- **Peaceful**: Disagreements and misbehavior are handled without yelling or hitting.

- **Positive**: The general tone of interactions between family members is constructive.

- **Encouraging**: When someone is struggling, others find ways to provide hope and encouragement.

Envisioning the type of home you want to create is the first step in making it a reality. Answer the questions on the next page to get started. Come back and update your answers as you think of new ideas.

What qualities would you like in your ideal home?

_____

_____

_____

_____

Which of these qualities are currently missing from your home?

_____

_____

_____

_____

What is one change you could make that would positively affect how your home feels?

_____

_____

_____

_____

Setting a Positive Tone

Parents play a lead role in setting the overall tone in their families. Parents whose overall tone tends to be negative often have homes filled with stress and tension. On the other hand parents who use a more positive approach create calmer, happier homes.

Sometimes parents get in the habit of interacting with their children using negative statements and commands. Read the following statements one dad made to his children and think about how you would feel if you were a child hearing these remarks:

- *"You aren't going outside until you put sunscreen on."*

- *"Stop messing around with that!"*

- *"If you don't hurry up and get your shoes on, I'm not taking you."*

- *"You've already watched too much TV. You should not have turned it on again, now turn it off."*

- *"You're not eating dinner until you wash your hands."*

- *"You are dawdling and we're going to be late!"*

- *"Stop bugging your sister!"*

How do you feel after reading these statements? Let's look at how these same ideas could be expressed more positively:

- *"Feel free to go outside as soon as you put sunscreen on."*

- *"That could break so you can play with this instead."*

- *"I am leaving in two minutes. I'll be happy to take you if have your shoes on."*

- *"Your TV time is up for today. Would you like to turn the TV off or would you like me to turn it off?"*

- *"Please wash your hands and then join us for dinner."*

- *"We're leaving in 5 minutes. Do you plan to be dressed or will you be taking your clothes in a bag?"*

- *"Your sister wants to be left alone right now. Do you want to play a game with me or go outside?"*

How do you feel now? The words we use make a huge difference! When we use more positive statements we demonstrate an unspoken

The words we choose create the tone they hear.

belief that our children are capable and are likely to choose appropriate behavior.

For the next few days, try paying attention to what you say to your children. If you hear yourself say something negative, figure out how you might communicate the same thing more positively. Here's some other questions to consider:

How did you greet your children first thing this morning?

_____

_____

_____

_____

When your children misbehave, what is your normal reaction?

_____

_____

_____

_____

When your children return home from school, what do you usually say to them?

_____

_____

_____

_____

Listening to Understand

Listening is one of those skills that really doesn't seem like it's all that difficult. Why then do so many children report that their parents don't listen to them?

Maybe it's because there are a lot of ways for parents to unintentionally stop conversations with their kids. For example, if your child comes home from school complaining that she didn't have anyone to play with at recess, these types of responses will probably leave her feeling unheard:

To understand your children, listen carefully.

- **Criticizing**: *"Well did you ask somebody to play with you?"*

- **Labeling**: *"A lot of times you act like a little dictator and other kids might not like that."*

- **Analyzing**: *"What did you do to try to get someone to play with you?"*

- **Diverting**: *"Why don't you go play outside with your sister and forget about it?"*

- **Reassuring**: *"I bet everyone in your class really likes you and they probably don't even realize they're leaving you out."*

- **Giving Advice**: *"I think you probably need to ask someone to play who is all by themselves."*

- **Lecturing**: *"When I was your age, I would just join whatever game anyone was playing. You really need to be brave and ask them to let you play. Tomorrow ask at least three children to play with you at recess."*

These types of responses are considered roadblocks to conversation because they tend to shutdown communication. It is extremely easy to accidentally use these roadblocks when talking to children.

If you want your children to feel heard, a better approach is to

- **Stop** what you are doing

- **Look** at your child

- Listen carefully - **pay attention to the body language**

- When your child is done speaking, **summarize** what you heard

When you summarize what you heard, you are giving your child the opportunity to clarify or correct your understanding.

Good listening takes time, patience and attention. You can't fully listen while also watching TV or working on the computer. Communication involves not only words but also body language, eye contact and tone of voice. So in order to understand your child's message, you need to both hear the words and watch how they are said.

Listening to our children while resisting the urge to jump in and solve the problem for them is not easy. However, often our children just want us to hear their concerns. They don't necessarily want our advice; they just want to be heard and understood.

Pick out five days where you will intentionally focus on really listening to your children. Write down something you learned each day from listening to your children.

1.

_____

_____

2.

_____

_____

3.

_____

_____

4.

_____

_____

5.

_____

_____

Showing Respect and Appreciation

Showing respect is a fundamental skill all children need to develop. As parents we can both model respectful behavior and guide our children in behaving respectfully.

One of the most basic forms of showing respect is to use "please" and "thank you". It is our job to teach our children to appropriately say "please" and "thank you". When children lack these basic courtesies, it causes problems.

Saying "please" and "thank you" shows respect.

For example, one aunt explained how hard she worked to find neat gifts for her three nephews. When opening the gifts they would often say things like

  "*I don't really like this.*"

  "*This isn't what I wanted.*"

Unfortunately, the parents did not step in to help their sons learn that these types of responses were hurtful and inappropriate.

At another holiday gathering children were wildly opening gifts without paying much attention to who the gift was from never mind actually thanking the person for the gift. The children threw aside each gift and anxiously started tearing the wrapping from the next gift. Again the parents failed to set up appropriate rules or expectations for the gift opening.

It's critical to teach children how to politely handle situations involving gifts. By discussing what to say under various situations ahead of time, children will be better prepared to act graciously even when receiving a gift they really aren't excited about.

It can also be helpful to agree on a gentle reminder signal, like a light touch on the ear, if children forget to say thank you.

There are many daily opportunities for children to practice saying "please" and "thank you":

- Asking for things to be passed at meal time

- When leaving a friend's house

- Making a request for help

Use situations like these to help your children practice their skills.

How well do you feel each of your children does in expressing appreciation?

_____

_____

_____

_____

If your children forget to say thank you, how would they like you to remind them?

_____

_____

_____

_____

What other expectations and values do you have around your children showing respect?

_____

_____

_____

_____

_____

_____

Dealing with Control Issues

Everyone likes control over their lives. Parents often create power struggles when they try to control something that their children ultimately control. In her book, <u>Positive Discipline</u>, Jane Nelsen explains "Excessive control invites rebellion or resistance, instead of encouraging children to learn the skills these parents want to teach." [1]

Moments of frustration can lead parents to issuing commands to try to control their children's behavior. Any time we are ordering children to change their behavior we're not likely to succeed. Instead of producing the desired behavioral change, commands often lead to some type of resistance.

For example, when feeling stressed to leave on time, we may yell to our children "Hurry up! It's time to get going!" It can feel good to give commands because it seems like we have more control over a situation when we're shouting commands. However, children often resist being told what to do (interestingly, most adults also do not like being told what to do!).

Since children ultimately control their own behavior, commands like these are usually ineffective:

- *"Stop crying!"*

- *"No more whining."*

- *"Don't give me that look."*

- *"Go to sleep right now!"*

It is easy to fall into the parenting trap of using commands to try and control children's behavior. However, it is far more effective to tell children what we are going to do instead of what they have to do. We might declare *"I'm leaving in five minutes."* instead of saying *"Hurry up!"*

A dad was trying to change his 18-month-old daughter's diaper while she was crying and struggling to get away. When doing an unappealing task like changing a diaper, it's difficult to have a child who is resisting and making an unpleasant task even more unpleasant.

This dad responded by telling his daughter *"Stop crying!"* Not only did she not stop crying, her crying intensified. It was easy to relate to his frustration as well as his child's reaction.

In this case, the dad probably would have been more successful by empathizing with his daughter by saying something like *"I can see you're really upset. I'm going to change your diaper and then we will leave."* By acknowledging her feelings and telling her what he was going to do, he could avoid telling her what she had to do.

When children are given appropriate control, they have little need to rebel.

Sometimes in the heat of the moment, we don't do our best parenting. It's helpful to reflect on how we wish we would have handled the situation. We are likely to have a second chance in the near future to handle a similar situation in a better way!

What are some examples of things your child controls? What do you control?

Children Control	Parent Controls
The food they choose to eat.	*The food that is purchased from the store.*

What is one thing you currently control that you could let your child control?

_____

_____

How will you turn control over to your child?

_____

_____

_____

_____

Giving Children Choices

Most parenting books discuss the power of giving children choices – and this one is no exception! Choices are a wonderful way to give children control while helping them learn about the consequences of their decisions.

One of our parenting goals is to ensure our children have solid decision making skills and are prepared to make serious decisions by the time they are about 12-years-old. This is critical because when our children become teens, they will start making serious decisions when we are not around.

Life is the sum of all your choices. ~Albert Camus

By giving children lots of choices when they are young, they'll be practicing making decisions and anticipating the consequences of those decisions. Our job as parents is so much easier when our children make wise decisions on their own.

Giving Choices Reduces Rebellion

When parents try to control their children's behavior, the result is often children who rebel. Rebelling is a way to resist their parents attempt to control them.

In her book <u>Wonderful Ways to Love a Child</u>, Judy Ford states "A child who trusts you to respect his independence has little need to rebel. The most rebellious and depressed adults are those who, as children, were the most strictly controlled. They were not allowed to find their own identity or make their own choices. Right or wrong, they were forced to dutifully follow their parent's authority."[2]

Cooperation Increases with Choices

Giving young children choices can make them far more cooperative. One mom was battling with her son over usingthe bathroom. One day instead of telling him to go use the bathroom she asked him "Do you want to gallop or walk to the bathroom?" She was surprised that he galloped to the bathroom without arguing!

Older children are also more agreeable when they have input into decisions that matter to them. For example, if teens get to choose their household chores, they're more likely to get their chores done with minimal grumbling!

By the time teens are graduating from high school, they will need to make important choices about what to do next in their lives. The more practice they've had making choices all along, the more capable they will be of thinking through this critical decision.

Here are some examples of turning commands into choices:

Commands	Choices
Go take your bath.	Do you want to take a bath upstairs or downstairs?
Do your homework.	Would you like to do your homework before dinner or after dinner?
Get dressed.	Would you prefer to get dressed at home or at preschool?
Go practice the piano.	You are welcome to practice the piano with the door shut or the door open.
Brush your teeth.	You can either brush your teeth or ask me to help you brush them.

Try giving your children lots of choices and write down some of the choices you gave them.

_____

_____

_____

_____

_____

How did your children handle these choices?   What do you think they learned?

_____

_____

_____

_____

Helping Children Solve Their Own Problems

When children come to us with a problem, it can be tempting to just solve the problem for them. However, if we want them to learn to solve similar problems in the future, it is better to guide them through finding a solution.

In her book, Easy to Love, Difficult to Discipline, Becky Bailey describes a process to help children solve their own problems[3]. She uses the acronym **PEACE** to make the steps easier to remember:

1. Discern who owns the **p**roblem.

2. Offer **e**mpathy to the child.

3. **A**sk the child to think, "What do you think you are going to do?"

4. Offer **c**hoices and suggestions.

5. **E**ncourage the child to come up with his own solution.

Remember to begin by connecting with empathy before working towards a solution.

Let's look at an example of using this process.   Suppose 4-year-old Ben runs to us crying because his 2-year-old sister Anna has knocked down his block structure. Here's how it might go:

1. We realize this is Ben's problem.

2. We show empathy by hugging Ben and saying *"I can see you're really sad. I know how hard you worked on building that."*

3. We ask Ben *"What do you think you are going to do?"*

4. Ben comes up with one idea; he wants to hit his sister. We quickly ask what is likely to happen if he does that! He decides not to do this but doesn't know what else to do. We offer the idea that he could build with the blocks in his room with the door shut. Ben rejects this idea because he wants to build in the living room. We suggest he could build when Anna is napping. Ben also rejects this idea.

5. We say *"I'm sure you'll find a good solution."* We've given him a couple ideas and we are leaving him with the responsibility for coming up with his own solution.

Here's one more example of using this process. This time let's pretend our 10-year-old daughter comes to us upset because she's forgotten her math assignment at school and it's due tomorrow. Here's how we might handle it:

1. We remember this is our daughter's problem since it's her homework.

2. We show empathy by saying *"I can understand why you are upset."*

3. We ask her *"What do you think you are going to do?"*

4. She's thought about going back to school to get it but she knows the teacher is already gone and the classroom door is locked. She doesn't know what else to do. We suggest calling a classmate to see if she can get a copy of the homework. When we ask her how this might work out, she replies that she's going to try giving Sara a call.

5. We say *"Great! I hope she can give you a copy of the homework or read off the problems to you."* We leave it up to her to call Sara and resolve the problem.

Once again we are guiding our child through the problem without providing the solution or insisting on what she should do.

How could you have used this process to guide your child through a recent problem?

_____

_____

_____

_____

The next time your child comes to you with a problem, use the process and write down what happened.

_____

_____

_____

_____

Giving Children Responsibilities

As children grow older, they are continually ready for new responsibilities (although they probably won't be asking for these new responsibilities!). From getting dressed to preparing a meal, kids need increasing responsibilities in order to grow into competent adults.

Children are often capable of more responsibility than we give them. When parents take on responsibilities which their children really should be handling, these parents are likely to feel overwhelmed and underappreciated.

Allow children to do what they are capable of doing.

One mom complained about all the extra work she was doing now that her 3rd and 6th graders were back in school. In just one day, she did all these extra tasks after they arrived home from school:

- Dumped out the kid's backpacks and sorted through papers.

- Reviewed graded schoolwork with the children.

- Worked on making dinner while being interrupted numerous times to help with homework.

- Ran to the store to buy purple shirts after the kids announced that they needed to wear purple tomorrow for Spirit Day.

- Packed forms, supplies and planners into each child's backpack.

- Spent 10 minutes looking for library books due the next day.

- Packed lunches for the next day.

- Did a load of laundry after one child reported having no clean socks.

- Yelled at the kids to GO TO BED NOW!

- Got youngest a drink of water.

Mom then collapsed into bed. Anyone would be exhausted after a day like that!

It is very easy for parents to take on responsibilities that their children could be handling. What tasks do you think this mom could let her children handle? Looking at someone else's situation can sometimes provide insight for our own situation.

Are there tasks you're doing for your children that they could be doing?

_____

_____

_____

_____

_____

What is one new responsibility your child is ready to take on?

_____

_____

_____

_____

_____

How will you respond if your child complains and doesn't want this new responsibility?

_____

_____

_____

_____

_____

Developing Children's Empathy

Children are not born with empathy. They are born with the capacity to have empathy but it only develops under certain conditions. Parents play a critical role in developing their children's empathy.

In their book, <u>Born for Love: Why Empathy is Essential - and Endangered</u>, Perry and Szalavitz write "The essence of empathy is the ability to stand in another's shoes, to feel what it's like there and to care about making it better if it hurts."[4] They document numerous cases where children have not experienced adequate empathy while growing up. These kids' behavior towards others also reflects a lack of empathy which often leads to serious problems.

The great gift of human beings is that we have the power of empathy.

-   Meryl Streep

Three key things you can do to develop your children's empathy are:

Key 1: Show empathy when responding to their behavior.

Children learn to be empathetic by being treated with empathy. This begins when they are babies with loving adults responding to their cries and needs. Soothing young children when they are upset lays the foundation for their own development of empathy.

Older children learn empathy when you respond to their behavior in a caring way rather than with anger. Instead of yelling "How could you do that?" or "What were you thinking?" respond in a way that demonstrates you understand what your child is going through. For example, if your child spilled juice, you might say "Oops! That's unfortunate. Let me know if you need any help cleaning it up."

Reflecting your child's feelings is another way of showing empathy. If your child has angrily thrown her math book down, you could say "I can see you're frustrated. I get frustrated too when I'm having trouble doing something."

Expressing empathy puts you and your child on the same side of the problem. When you show compassion and understanding, your child is in a better position for thinking about a solution to the problem.

Key 2: Demonstrate genuine empathy.

When using empathy, it needs to come from your heart. If it doesn't sound genuine, children will quickly see through it as fake empathy.

One mom of two teens complained that she tried to be empathetic to their problems but it only seemed to make them mad. She went on to explain that she would often respond to their problems by saying "bummer". Instead of feeling genuinely understood, they felt angry because it seemed like she was belittling them.

To see a situation from your child's viewpoint, it can help to think of a situation where you've experienced something similar to what your child is experiencing. For example, if you've ever ordered a meal at a restaurant and then regretted your choice when the meal actually came, you can understand how your child might feel in a similar situation like the following one.

Pretend you asked your child, "What would you like for breakfast: cereal, pancakes or toast?" Suppose your child chooses cereal but when you place the cereal in front of her she says "I changed my mind. I want pancakes." You may be tempted to yell "You asked for cereal; I got you cereal; Now eat it!"

Instead you could show more understanding by responding with something like "Now that you have your cereal you're disappointed you didn't chose pancakes. Tomorrow morning you can choose pancakes." If she becomes upset, it's better to acknowledge her feelings again with something like "I realize you are upset." instead of "Stop complaining and eat!"

Key 3: Discuss other people's perspectives

Reading books can help develop understanding of other people's points of view. Perry and Szalavitz talk about the importance of reading to children and discussing the actions and feelings of the characters. "When you read to them or discuss books, ask what they think the characters are thinking and feeling. Point out facial expressions and body language and talk about what these mean."

You can have this same type of discussion with the events happening in your children's lives. For example, if a new student has joined your child's class, you can talk to your child about how it must feel to be a new student in the class and to not know anyone yet. By trying to understand how this new student is feeling, your child may be inspired to find ways to help this new student feel more comfortable.

When you help your children see the world from different viewpoints you help them develop their empathy. When children can feel empathy for others, they are far less likely to engage in behaviors like bullying.

By treating your children with empathy and guiding them to treat others that way, you are helping to build a more caring community for everyone. This is a very worthy goal indeed!

Practice responding to your children with empathy. Write down what you did and how it felt.

_____

_____

_____

Learning through Chores

We have until our children are about 18-years-old to teach them all the basic skills they'll need to live on their own. That's a lot of teaching! Doing household chores is a great way for kids to learn the skills needed to run a household.

It's also important for children to learn that being part of a family means helping out with household tasks. We do not want our children growing up seeing us as their personal servants!

Chores build competence and confidence.

Starting Chores Early

Starting chores when children are young and enthusiastic is great timing. Most preschoolers are not very good at chores but they are often eager to help. When parents give their preschoolers some simple chores and start teaching them how to do more complicated ones, they are on the road to enabling their children to be significant contributors to the family.

One mom explained she is teaching her 5-year-old twins how to do the laundry. Although she still needs to provide some guidance, the boys are so proud they know what buttons to push and how to do a load of laundry! Mastering new household skills builds self-confidence in children and starts building appreciation for what needs to be done to keep the household running.

Choosing Chores

It can be helpful to list out all the tasks that need to be done to keep your family going (including things like going to work to earn money, paying bills, providing rides). Next, sit down with your kids to discuss how to divide up these tasks.

It's important for each person to understand their chores. Some families post daily chore lists in the kitchen. Others work together on chores on a certain day of the week.

Paying for Extra Chores

One way to allow children to earn money is to pay them for doing extra chores in addition to their normal ones. It's a great way to get work done and for our children to earn money for the special things they would like.

Our children earned a trampoline by each doing 100 extra chores. It took them almost a year to accomplish this and they were extremely proud when they finished earning the trampoline!

What chores do your children have?

_____

_____

_____

_____

How do your children know what chores are their responsibility?

_____

_____

_____

_____

What is the time frame for them completing their chores?

_____

_____

_____

_____

What happens if the chores aren't done?

_____

_____

_____

Focusing on Positive Behavior

Since we tend to get more of whatever we focus on, we definitely want to focus on our children's positive behavior! Simply paying attention to children when they are behaving well will increase the likelihood that they'll repeat that behavior.

Some parents accidentally provide plenty of attention only when their children are misbehaving. These children quickly learn that when they are throwing food on the floor or slamming doors, they will get their parent's attention. Interestingly, children will repeat behaviors that get them attention even if it is negative attention.

We get more of whatever we focus on.

Commenting specifically on what you like is a way to give positive attention:

- *"It was kind of you to share the truck with John."*

- *"Thank you for unloading the dishwasher without even being asked."*

- *"I'm impressed with how quickly you got dressed."*

- *"I appreciate your help in putting the napkins on the table."*

Likewise, ignoring negative behavior helps reduce it. If a behavior is irritating but not dangerous or cruel, try ignoring it.

For example, parents who ignore their children's fighting may be pleasantly surprised to see a reduction in sibling rivalry. Parents who attempt to intervene and stop the fighting often get the opposite results.

When we focus on children's good behavior, we help them recognize their positive attributes. Some virtues to encourage include:

- **Self-control**: staying in control of emotions and behavior

- **Manners**: behaving politely

- **Respect**: showing consideration for the worth of someone or something

- **Generosity**: willingness to give money, help or time to others

- **Compassion**: understanding the suffering of others and wanting to do something about it

- **Responsibility**: being reliable in one's obligations

- **Honesty**: being truthful, sincere and fair

- **Acceptance**: having an objective attitude toward other's ideas and practices that differ from your own

- **Integrity**: sticking to moral and ethical principles and values

- **Perseverance**: persisting in a course of action, belief or purpose

- **Fairness**: acting in a just way, sharing appropriately

Which virtues would you most like to work on developing in your children?

_____

_____

_____

_____

Which of these virtues will you focus on first? Second?

_____

_____

What ideas do you have for helping your children build these virtues?

_____

_____

_____

_____

_____

Providing Love and Approval

Our children want our love and approval. They need to feel like they belong in our family and are appreciated for who they are. When we let them know how much they mean to us, they are more likely to feel loved and act in positive ways.

Children pay great attention to what their parents focus on. If they hear a lot of praise for their accomplishments but not a lot of appreciation for being themselves, they may conclude that it's their achievements that matter most.

All children want to belong and to be loved.

Parents can unintentionally reinforce this thinking by focusing on things like:

- Grades instead of effort

- Winning instead of playing the game fairly and to the best of one's ability

- Being the top performer instead of achieving a personal best

- Doing something perfectly instead of doing as well as possible

One mom said that her 25-year-old daughter confessed that growing up she always tried to hide her struggles and failures from her mom. She felt her mom wanted her to be perfect and didn't want to disappoint her. This mom had never intended to give her daughter this message and was very surprised to learn that she felt this way.

What you notice about your children and how you say it matters greatly. When you make comments about their character, they are more likely to realize it's who they are not what they do that matters most.

These types of comments reinforce positive character traits:

- *"You were really generous to share that with your sister."*

- *"You are great at cheering your teammates on!"*

- *"Your smile always brightens up my day."*

- *"I am impressed with how hard you worked on that paper."*

Another important way of demonstrating love is to hug our kids and say *"I love you."* Some parents find this easier to do than others. It gets more challenging as children become teens and aren't the cuddly toddlers they once were. It's still important though even if they act like it's not!

What characteristics do you admire in each of your children?

_____

_____

_____

_____

_____

How do you let your children know what you admire in them?

_____

_____

_____

_____

_____

When is the last time you told your children that you love them?

_____

_____

What other ways do you let them know you love them?

_____

_____

_____

Encouraging Self-Motivation

How can we motivate our children to work harder in school, in a sport or in practicing an instrument? Will the promise of a reward for practicing the piano help our child practice more? Or will the threat of punishment be more effective? When we try to motivate our children to work harder, we can often end up feeling frustrated by the results.

Understanding Internal Motivation

Ideas about motivation are changing as new research teases out some of the key elements. According to Daniel Pink's latest book, <u>Drive: The Surprising Truth About What Motivates Us</u>, trying to motivate children using external rewards and punishment is a mistake.[5] The secret for motivating children to high performance lies in allowing their own internal drives direct their behavior.

Pink describes three elements of true motivation:

- **Autonomy** - the need to direct our own lives

- **Mastery** - the desire to make progress in one's work

- **Purpose** - the ability to positively impact ourselves and our world

For example, if you want your child to practice the piano more, try allowing her to choose when to practice, what music to focus on and where to perform that will bring delight to someone else.

Trying to Control Too Much

When we try to motivate our children, it sometimes backfires as they dig in their heels and refuse to buckle under the pressure. By attempting to exert control over our children's behavior, we are reducing their autonomy - one of the key elements of internal motivation.

One mom was describing her frustration in getting her daughter to practice the piano. No matter how hard she tried her daughter sat on the piano bench refusing to put her fingers on the keys. This is a typical control battle and one that mom is likely to lose since her daughter ultimately controls what she does with her fingers!

How do we know when we've stepped over the line and are trying to control too much of our children's behavior? Luckily children are pretty good at letting us know when we've stepped over that line. If you hear your child saying any of the following, you're probably over the line:

- "You're not the boss of me!"

- "I'm not going to do that!"

"Nothing great was ever achieved without enthusiasm."

-- Ralph Waldo Emerson

- "You can't make me."

- "Why do you always get to choose?"

At this point it is wise to take a step back and look at what we are trying to accomplish and consider other approaches.

Motivating to Perfection

Psychologist Robert W. Hill of Appalachian State University found that when people are trying hard because of their own desire for excellence, this effort can lead to greater satisfaction and mental health. However, if the pressure to perform is coming from others, it's likely to lead to dissatisfaction and reduced well-being.

In the article "The Two Faces of Perfection", Hill is quoted as saying "Kids need to get the message, 'You need to have high standards, but you don't need to be perfect.' If you have unreachable goals and you're constantly dissatisfied with yourself, you can be miserable. Unequivocally, you don't want a parent who is constantly criticizing, so the child develops a self-scrutiny that always finds fault with their own performance."[6]

While we all want our children to try hard and make good choices, in order to accomplish this we need to allow them to practice making those choices. Some of the choices they make will not be so good and that will give them an opportunity to learn from their mistakes.

By giving our children the chance to develop their self-motivation, we encourage them to grow and find their own internal strengths.

When are your children the most motivated? What is it they will gladly do without being asked?

_____

_____

_____

Ask them what they do to motivate themselves when they don't feel like doing something.

_____

_____

_____

Setting Limits Around Media Usage

When parents discuss how much media they allow their children, the answers vary wildly. Some parents have very strict time restrictions on their children's media viewing while others give their children more control over the time they spend on media.

How do you know when your child is getting too much media?

One mom knew she needed to allow less video game time when her 7-year-old son started not wanting play outside or do things with the family preferring his video game instead. He was so attached to playing his video game that he often pitched a fit when he was told the game had to go off. His games didn't have a good way to save the game for later so he was reluctant to stop playing and lose his place in the game.

She decided to reduce his video game playing to one hour twice a week. She started giving him a 10 minute warning before his hour was up. When the 10 minutes were up, he could either choose to shut the game off or she would turn the power off. It only took a couple times of turning the power off to get him to shut the game down in time.

The Kaiser Family Foundation's 2010 report showed kids 8 - 18 averaged spending 7 hours and 38 minutes with media each day.

What are signs that digital usage is becoming a problem?

If your children are exhibiting these types of behaviors, it's time to think about reducing the time they spend on media:

- Spending less and less time with family and friends

- Difficulty focusing on the present moment due to craving video game or cellphone

- Developing health issues such as Carpel Tunnel Syndrome, eye strain, weight gain, backaches

- Withdrawing from sports, hobbies and social interactions

- Losing sleep due to gaming, texting

- Acting irritable or discontent when not using digital items

- Declining grades in school, missing school

- Talking and thinking obsessively about the digital activity

- Denying or minimizing any negative consequences

What do the experts recommend?

Hilarie Cash, psychotherapist and co-author of Video Games & Your Kids, makes the following recommendations for personal screen time (computer, TV, video games). This time does not include computer time needed for homework.[7]

- Under 2-years-old: no screen time

- Preschool: 1 - 2 hours/day

- Elementary: 2 hours/day

- Junior/Senior High: 2 - 3 hours/day

She also recommends no TV, internet or gaming consoles in children's rooms. The primary problem with having these devices in children's bedrooms is that parents have more difficulty monitoring what's going on.

If you feel your child is addicted to video games and will react extremely to having limits set, it is wise to seek help from a professional counselor or psychologist.

How much time are your children currently spending on media each day?

_____

_____

_____

_____

If your children are old enough, discuss reasonable limits on media and how your family will monitor and set those limits. What limits did you decide to set?

_____

_____

_____

_____

Talking About the Birds and the Bees

One more thing on your to-do list as a parent ... talk to your kids about relationships, love and sex! Did you know that experts recommend the conversation should be started by age five and that by age seven children should have a basic understanding about the facts of reproduction? Children with this information are less likely to be the victims of sexual abuse.

Starting the Conversation

When we start the dialog when children are young, it's easier to continue it as they grow older. Although we may be uncomfortable discussing the basics of sex with our young children, they typically are not embarrassed. One way to get started is to read an age appropriate book together.

Plan to have many small talks over the years.

There are many excellent books on sexuality for all age groups. You can find a number of these books on the Priceless Parenting web site:

http://www.PricelessParenting.com/BooksOnSexuality.aspx

Most young children are interested in their bodies and the differences between boys and girls. Understanding private parts and who has a right to touch or see those parts is important information for them to have.

Continuing the Conversation

As children reach puberty, they need information about the changes their bodies will be going through. Although some children will learn this information in school, it's still important for parents to also be part of the conversation.

When our children have questions or concerns, we want them to be able to come to us. They will be more comfortable approaching us if we have been engaged in an ongoing dialog over the years.

Discussing Our Values About Sexuality

By clarifying our own values and beliefs about sexuality and relationships, we are in a better position to discuss these issues with our children. We can help prepare our children to make better decisions in their relationships by discussing our values.

Teens report wanting to hear more from their parents regarding relationships and sex. Unfortunately, without enough information teens often underestimate the likelihood of contracting a sexually transmitted infection or becoming pregnant.

When a teen becomes pregnant, the parents pay a heavy price. The U.S. Census 2000 figures show that 2.4 million grandparents had primary responsibility for raising their grandchildren. While these aren't all cases of teenage pregnancy, this data certainly motivated me to talk to my two teenagers about sexuality and the incredible responsibility involved in having a baby.

What discussions have you had with your children on sexuality? What are they ready for next?

_____

_____

_____

_____

_____

What messages do you want to give your teens about relationships, sex, birth control, abstinence?

_____

_____

_____

_____

_____

What rules do you think are important to have around dating?

_____

_____

_____

_____

Teaching Financial Responsibility

Providing an allowance is a wonderful way to begin teaching children about money. It is also a great way to give children some control over spending decisions and avoid arguments in the store!

Save Money - Give Your Child an Allowance

It may seem counterintuitive to give your child an allowance in order to save money but it works! Anything extra your children would like at the store can now be their responsibility to purchase. When they ask to buy something, you can say *"Sure, as long as you have enough money."*

Children think longer and harder when spending their own money rather than their parents' money.

By the time children are 3 or 4-years-old, most are ready for an allowance. Having their own money helps children learn about the value of money. They learn important skills like delaying purchases until they've saved enough money.

Allowing Kids to Make Spending Mistakes

A dad told the story of how he was shopping with his 6-year-old son and his son decided he really wanted to buy a toy car with his allowance money. The car he wanted was flimsy and the dad was fairly sure that it wouldn't last long before it broke. The dad mentioned his concerns to his son but still allowed his son to make his own choice on whether or not to buy it.

Well his son bought the car. Within a week of having it, the front wheels broke off. Instead of saying *"I told you so"*, the dad helped his son glue it back together. Although it wasn't quite as good as before, the son thanked his dad for helping him fix it. This boy's respect for his dad grew along with some wisdom about buying cheap toys.

Opening Bank Accounts and Learning About Credit

It's helpful to get a bank account started when children are young so they can begin saving for their future. When they are older, we can help them get checkbooks and learn about keeping track of their account balance.

When children are in their late teens, we can start explaining the idea of credit. It is especially important to discuss credit cards and interest payments.

One dad was shocked to learn his 25-year-old daughter didn't realize that when she made the minimum credit card payment she was going to be charged a steep interest rate on the remaining balance. She quickly learned this point when she saw her next credit card statement!

How do you handle allowance for your children?

_____

_____

_____

_____

_____

What things are your children responsible for purchasing for themselves?

_____

_____

_____

_____

_____

How do you handle situations where your children do not have enough money to purchase something they want?

_____

_____

_____

_____

_____

Making Time to be Together

Being able to spend fun times together with our children is part of what makes being a parent so rewarding. It also shows our children how important they are to us. However, it can be challenging to take time to have fun.

Postponing the Most Important Things

As parents our days can easily be filled to overflowing with all the tasks that are required to keep our families running: making meals, doing dishes, driving kids to activities, washing clothes and working.

These are certainly not the most important things in our lives but they can quickly take over our most of our time. It's easy to say things like:

- *"I'll play a game with the kids tomorrow."*

- *"We'll go for a bike ride together soon."*

- *"I'll bake some cookies with them when I have more time."*

The things that are the most important to us are also often the ones that are the easiest to postpone. The problem is that sometimes we delay so long that we miss the opportunity.

Our children will not want to have a tea party or play catch with us forever. They quickly grow up. If we want to share special times with our children, we must intentionally carve out the time to do these things.

At the end of your life, what do you want your children to remember about you? Certainly I don't want my kids' strongest memory to be "Mom always kept the bathrooms really clean!" However, if I want my kids to remember special times we shared together, then I need to take time today to play with them, listen to them and be there for them.

Carving Out Daily Time Together

Children need our ongoing attention. If we don't give them enough attention, they may misbehave just to get some attention.

One mom explained when she came home from work each day the first thing she did was change into more comfortable clothes. Her 4-year-old son typically managed to get in trouble or throw a tantrum while she was changing her clothes.

She decided to try a new routine. When she came home, she spent a few minutes playing with him before she changed her clothes. This made a huge, positive difference!

Spending fun time together creates wonderful memories.

What activities do you most enjoy doing with your children?

_____

_____

_____

_____

When is the last time you did these activities?

_____

_____

_____

_____

Discuss with your children something special they would like to do.   When will you do it?

_____

_____

_____

_____

Chapter 2:
Parenting Behaviors to Avoid

Priceless® Parenting

Some parenting techniques may work well in the short term but lead to long term problems. This chapter we will review some of the parenting behaviors that are best to avoid.

Negative Techniques Don't Feel Good

You've undoubtedly heard the saying "The only person you can change is yourself." It's both wise and true! The part not mentioned is that changing your behavior does affect others. When parents positively change their behavior, they may be amazed at the equally positive changes in their children's behavior.

One way we can make positive changes in our parenting is to stop certain behaviors. It is easy to get into the habit of using negative techniques, like yelling, in response to our children's misbehavior. However, by refraining from yelling, hitting, nagging and lecturing, you will see wonderful changes in your relationship with your children.

Negative Techniques Work

In this chapter we'll look at common parenting behaviors that are best to avoid. Some of these behaviors, like bribing children, are very tempting since they may immediately correct a behavior. However, the long term results are poor.

How do you make your kids feel?

When we use a negative technique to try to change our children's behavior, it often works in the short term but typically doesn't leave us feeling good as parents. When we show respect to our children, we make them feel appreciated and loved. We also model how to treat others with respect.

Think back to your last interaction with your children when you were dealing with a problem.

- How do you think they felt afterwards?

- How did you feel?

- Is there a different way you'd like to handle a situation like this in the future?

If we want to build warm, loving relationships with our children, paying attention to these feelings can provide important guidance.

"I've learned that people will forget what you said, people will forget what you did, but people will never forget how you made them feel."
-- Maya Angelou

Hitting Children

Parents who spank or hit their kids may do so because it temporarily stops a behavior. While hitting children may have the short term benefit of stopping a behavior, there are longer term negative effects including:

- Increasing children's aggression

- Increasing children's desire to get away from punishing parent

- Teaching children to hit others

- Deteriotating children's relationship with their parents

Learn ways to set limits without resorting to hitting.

While it is very important for parents to set limits with their children, ideally it should be done in a way that helps children learn from their mistakes. We'll explore these ideas more in the next chapter.

Hitting Older Children

An exasperated dad of a 12-year-old boy told me *"I wish I could just beat him! That would straighten him out."* He went on to explain that as a child he had been beaten for misbehaving and he quickly learned not to misbehave. His son had just been suspended from school that day for fighting and he was at wits end trying to figure out how to deal with this boy's behavior.

When you're experiencing this level of challenge and frustration with your child, it's time to get some outside help. Hitting your child is definitely not the answer.

In Dr. Michael Bradley's book, <u>Yes, Your Teen is Crazy</u>, he explains why hitting an adolescent is a very bad idea:

"You are now officially discharged from the army of hitters of children (if you were ever in that group). As the parent of an adolescent, you must assume the status of conscientious objector. You don't do violence anymore. You don't hit, smack, butt, throttle, jab, or even look like you might ever do any of these things. You draw an invisible circle around your kid and you never cross over that line uninvited.

You do this for two reasons. The first is that hitting doesn't work anyway. The second is that smacking an adolescent is an experience very much like whacking at an old stick of dynamite. Often, it doesn't explode right away, but when it does, it will demolish everything around it. The question is why would anyone whack at a stick of dynamite or at an adolescent?"[1]

Yelling at Children

When parents attending my classes talk about which of their behaviors they'd most like to change, the most common response is that they'd like to stop yelling at their kids. It is very natural to yell when we're angry; nobody has to teach us how to do that!

Begging for Ice Cream

One mom told me how exasperated she was while driving her 10-year-old son to Baskin Robbins to order cake for his upcoming birthday party. Her son started pleading with her to get an ice cream cone at Baskin Robbins. Mom said he couldn't have one since he had just had ice cream yesterday.

Ranting and raving leaves everyone feeling bad.

He didn't give up hope and instead kept asking her if he could please have an ice cream cone. Completely fed up, she pulled over and stepped out of the car for a few minutes explaining she needed a break from his behavior.   After getting back in the car, he soon asked her again about the ice cream!

Feeling quite angry now, she yelled at him for continuing to ask after she had already told him no. By the end of her rant, he was crying. Needless to say, this wasn't exactly the pleasant outing she had envisioned.

Alternative Parenting Responses

We don't always do our best parenting in the heat of the moment. The good news is that when we realize we haven't handled a parenting situation in the ideal way, we can reflect on what happened and figure out what we would like to do differently in the future.

Sometimes we're too close to the situation or still too upset to see any alternatives. If this is the case, it can be helpful to ask other parents for ideas. It's always easier to see choices when you're not the parent involved!

What suggestions might you give this mom?

Ideally we are looking for a response that models both self-control and treating others with respect. We also need to be able to follow through with whatever we say we are going to do. For example, if he begs again after we said we would turn around and go home, then that's what we need to do.

In Chapter 3 we'll discuss other possibilities for handling this type of situation.

Nagging and Ordering Children Around

It's easy to get in the habit of nagging children and expressing frustration when they don't quickly obey. When we nag children, the unspoken belief is that unless we give them continual reminders of what they should be doing, they will forget. However, making requests multiple times does not increase the chance children will do what we are asking; it actually teaches them how to tune us out.

Eliminating Nagging from the Morning Routine

Do you ever find yourself rushing around in the morning desperately trying to get your kids off to school? Feeling rushed and hassled first thing in the morning is not a good way to start a day! Unfortunately many parents and children report this is exactly how they feel in the mornings.

Replace nagging with giving children responsibility.

How can we change our behavior so that mornings feel calm instead of chaotic? It can help to take a step back and look at what needs to get done in the mornings and how we want to interact with our children.

Adding Stress by Nagging and Ordering

One thing that adds to morning stress is when parents feel they need to give their kids lots of orders to get them out the door on time:

- *"Eat your breakfast."*

- *"Brush your teeth."*

- *"Get dressed right now!"*

- *"Remember to bring your clarinet."*

Whenever we order our kids to do something, we are setting ourselves up for a possible power struggle. If they choose not to follow our orders, we're likely to feel angry and want to increase the pressure in an attempt to force them to change their behavior.

Orders also send the unspoken message "You need me to help you remember what to do." This is not quite the message we want to be sending! Instead it's better if we can help our children find their own ways to remember. For example, our children could create a chart of everything that needs to be done each morning and then check the chart to make sure everything is done.

By turning more responsibility over to our children, we can relieve ourselves from having to police their morning routines. This can be scary as mistakes will undoubtedly be made. However, children quickly learn from their mistakes and become more competent.

Doing Things for Children that They Can Do for Themselves

When we do things for our children that they are capable of doing themselves, we often end up feeling exhausted and underappreciated. When we expect children to do things they know how to do, they develop responsibility.

Never mind, I'll do it!

As parents we can find ourselves frustrated by the lack of speed our children have in getting tasks done. When we are tired of waiting or really need something done right now, we may find ourselves saying *"Never mind, I'll do it!"*

Allow children to do whatever they are capable of doing.

It often takes less time and energy to simply do it ourselves. However, when we jump in and do something our children should be doing, we are stealing the opportunity for them to increase their self-discipline and sense of responsibility.

What do our children think when they hear us say things like *"Never mind, I'll do it"?* Perhaps thoughts like:

- I can get out of doing work if I simply delay long enough.

- Dad is mad at me but at least I don't have to do it.

- I'm kind of lazy.

Since this response isn't sending positive messages to our children, it's something to avoid doing.

Taking Over Tasks Children Can Do

One dad described being so frustrated with his 5-year-old's slowness in getting dressed that he finally took over and dressed his son. In his anger he scolded his son saying he was acting like a baby and shouldn't need help getting dressed.

What thoughts was this boy probably having about himself in this situation? What thoughts was he having about his dad?

Another approach this dad could have taken was to give his son the choice of getting dressed at home or taking his clothes in a bag and getting dressed at school. This simple technique was first described by Jane Nelsen in her Positive Discipline book. It was something she tried with her own son and it worked so well she shared it![2]

Allowing our children to accomplish their own tasks in their own way is a gift which will help them grow.

Bribing Children

Why do parents turn to bribing their kids to behave? One reason is that it often gets the desired results right away.

One mom told me about how her son was begging her to watch a Star Wars movie that they had bought the previous night. They were planning to watch it as a family the following night but that wasn't soon enough for him! He kept on asking to watch it and proceeded to try to persuade her even when she was on the phone.

Bribing solves a short term problem while creating a long term problem.

Since her phone call was for business and she really needed to complete the conversation, she took a quick break to promise her son an ice cream cone if he stopped bugging her. He immediately agreed and stopped nagging her!

While she achieved the desired behavior, he learned that nagging her may result in a treat. Do you think he'll try nagging her again?

Whatever behaviors we reward, we can expect to see more of those behaviors in the future!

Increasing the Reward

Another problem with bribing is that it doesn't address the underlying issue. For example, if you are shopping with a young child who is tired, you may be able to use bribery to temporarily get better behavior. However, the poor behavior is likely to quickly return since the child is still tired.

Once while shopping at Trader Joes I overheard a mom struggling with her young daughter who was sitting in the front of their shopping cart. Mom was agreeing "OK, I'll give you one money." The daughter whined "Nooooo, I want TWO monies!" Mom fished around her purse and handed her a couple coins. The daughter then yelled "That's not enough!" and began crying.

Mom begged her to please stop crying because she really needed to get this shopping done before they could go home. Mom was exasperated as her daughter continued to cry.

If you find yourself begging or bribing your kids to behave, it's time to find some better parenting approaches!

Threatening or Scaring Children

Another way we can get kids to quickly change their behavior is to threaten them. While it may work, we are eroding the trust our children have in us when we make threats like "If you don't shape up I'm just going to leave you here."

What Do Children Learn from Threats?

One Mom wrote that her 4-year-old daughter did not want to put on her shoes so they could leave McDonalds when it was time to go. She solved the problem by telling her daughter "*That's fine. I'll leave you here and the hobos will come and take you away.*" Her daughter immediately got her shoes on!

While scaring our kids may work in the short term, in the long term the consequences aren't so desirable. Since we really can't abandon them at McDonalds, our children learn that we won't necessarily follow through on what we say.

We are also showing that they can't always count on us to protect them. Are these really the messages we want our kids to be hearing?

Threatening children weakens their trust in us.

Replacing Threats with Promises

Another mom was exasperated with her preschool daughter after she pitched fit for 45 minutes upon learning that her little brother was going swimming while she was at preschool. When mom was completely fed up with the whining and crying, she threatened to let her daughter sit in her room all day missing both preschool and a dance class. Her daughter stopped crying and got ready for school.

In this case, the threat got the girl to stop her tantrum. But what if she would have continued? Does mom really want her daughter to have the choice of skipping school? Probably not.

The problem with threats is that we normally make them when we are angry and therefore threaten things that we really don't want carry through on. Instead of using a threat, mom could have used a promise when her daughter started protesting like "I know you are upset that you can't go swimming today. I'll be happy to take you swimming next week if I don't use up that energy listening to you whining and crying."

We want our children to be able to trust that we will follow through on what we say. Therefore, we want to avoid threats made in anger since those threats tend to be extreme and not well thought out. It is far better to choose promises we'd be happy to fulfill rather than angry threats that will deteriorate our relationship with our children.

Lecturing and Over Explaining

When we feel strongly about a topic, it's easy to launch into a lecture. Unfortunately, lecturing is typically not an effective way to get children's behavior to change.

For example, parents who feel passionate about their children trying hard in school may lecture them about the importance of studying hard. To the parents giving the lecture, it may feel like progress is being made. However, they may be very disappointed to find that their children still aren't getting their homework done even after carefully explaining the importance of doing homework!

Use fewer words to get better results.

Lecturing is not a Dialog

Lecturing is one-sided. Parents talk, children listen (or at least pretend to listen!). Parents tell their kids what they believe on a topic. However, since this isn't a discussion, the children don't usually get to voice their opinions and ideas.

At the end of a lecture, parents may think their children will now behave differently. If the children haven't responded, it's not clear how they intend to change or not change their behavior.

The parent giving the lecture may take the stance of being unquestionably correct. When that's the case, there is no room for questions or dialog because there is only one right answer.

People are far more commited to changing their behavior when they've been involved with the decision. Lectures don't allow this type of buy-in.

Over Explaining Provides Attention

When we explain to children at length about why a certain behavior is or is not appropriate, we are giving children lots of attention. Attention tends to reinforce behaviors so we may be encouraging the very behavior we want to stop!

One day I saw a couple was trying to convince their 5-year-old daughter to get in the car because it was time to leave the park. This girl did not want to go home.

Her parents carefully explained why they needed to go home. I walked by 30 minutes later and they were still explaining to her why they needed to go!

Battling Over Food

Eating is essential for our existence. Making meal times pleasant, instead of a battle ground, will greatly improve the precious time we spend together with our children.

Avoiding power struggles around eating

I heard one 9-year-old girl ask her dad "Why are you the boss of what I eat?" Her dad was carefully monitoring how much his daughter was eating and encouraging her to eat more in order to earn dessert.

Food battles make sharing meals together unpleasant.

This type of battle takes a toll on relationships plus makes meal time unpleasant. It is the parent's job to provide healthy food and to teach children why their bodies need healthy food. However, it is the children's job to decide what to eat and how much to eat. This is an essential skill for all children to develop.

If you want to set limits around food, tell the children what you are going to do or give them choices. For example:

- *"You're welcome to have the noodles I'm making for lunch or you can make yourself a sandwich."*

- *"I've put out carrots and grapes. Help yourself to as much of these as you'd like before dinner is ready."*

- *"We'll be leaving the restaurant in 5 minutes. Finish eating as much as you want so that you're not hungry before we eat again."*

Catering to Food Preferences

Parents can unitentionally create picky eaters by catering strongly to their children's preferences. Some of the ways parents can limit their children's palate include:

- Buying a single brand of food – for example, only buying Oroweat 12 Grain bread.

- Taking special meals for their children when they go over to someone else's house for dinner.

- Serving only food their children already like.

One high school girl reported she finally started trying new food when she took a trip with her high school class to Europe. She commented that being hungry was a very good motivator!

Saying "I told you so!" or "Because I said so!"

When we say things like "I told you so!", we are rubbing salt in the wound. If our children are suffering because they failed to follow our advice, it is far better to show compassion for their pain.

"Didn't I tell you this would happen?"

I saw a young boy walking home with his mother from school. He tripped on the bottom of his pants, fell, skinned his knee and burst into tears. His mother reminded him *"I told you this would happen. Those pants are too long for you."*

Her son would have felt more understood if she comforted him and showed compassion. Had she instead given him a hug and said something like "*Ow! That really hurt.",* she would have been on the same side of the problem as her son with his bad decision on the other side.

Nobody likes hearing "*I told you so*". It can be sometimes feel good to say it but it is far better for your relationship with that other person if you avoid saying it.

When you've been proven correct, don't mention it.

"Because I said so!"

Lucy angrily recalled a turning point in her relationship with her mom over 50 years ago. She was graduating from 9th grade and asked her mother if after the graduation ceremony she could spend the afternoon at a lake with some of her girlfriends. One of the other mothers was driving them to the lake and bringing lunch.

Her mom replied *"You're not going."* When Lucy asked her mom why she couldn't go, her response was *"Because I said so."*

Lucy was enraged with her mother's explanation. She angrily told her mother that she planned to go to the lake with her friends despite the fact her mother told her she couldn't go. When her mother asked for an explanation, Lucy replied *"Because I said so."* Lucy did go to the lake with her friends that day. Her relationship with her mother remained cool and unaffectionate for many years.

When parents declare to their children something will or will not happen *"because I said so"*, they are trying to use their authority to end the discussion. A better approach is to carefully listen to the child's request and ask questions to address any concerns you have before deciding. Providing respectful, thoughtful explanations for decisions helps maintain good relationships with our children even if the decision isn't the one they wanted.

Reacting Before Understanding

It's easy to react to our children's behavior before we really understand why they did or said something. Below is an example of this type of reaction along with an idea for a better approach.

One mom told the story of driving her 5-year-old son, Nick, home from preschool one day when he announced "John is an ass!" Taken aback by this inappropriate name calling, she responded to Nick "Good boys do not use language like that. You should never call anyone that name."

She then asked Nick why he said that. Nick explained that John was always asking him to play every day. She replied "That's a really nice thing that John is doing. You should be happy that he wants to play with you." That remark shutdown the conversation and Nick was now mad both at John and his mom.

Let's take a step back and see how this might have played out differently. In the dialog below, Mom ignores the inappropriate language and avoids telling Nick that he should be happy that John is asking him to play.

Seek first to understand and then to be understood.

-- Stephen R. Covey

Nick: "John is an ass!"

Mom: "You sound really angry."

Nick: "Yeah, he is always asking me to play with him every day."

Mom: "Why is that a problem?"

Nick: "Because sometimes I'm already playing a game with someone else and I don't want to stop in the middle of it."

Mom: "John wants you to stop what you are playing and go play with him."

Nick: "Yeah, but I don't want to."

Mom is now making headway in understanding why Nick is feeling angry with John. She's also helping Nick gain insight into the underlying issues. Once they truly understand the situation, they can brainstorm possible solutions.

Mom can always go back later and address Nick's choice of words. When Nick is calm, he'll be in a better frame of mind for considering other ways he could express his anger.

Breaking Promises

"But you promised!" It's easy to misinterpret a statement as a promise when no promise was intended. Being intentional about what is a promise and what is not can be helpful in avoiding misunderstandings.

When you do make a promise, especially to a child, it is important to follow through with what you promised.

Promises to Children

I attended a seminar where the leader asked us to think back to a situation from our childhood where someone broke a promise to us. Each of us was able to vividly remember a situation; it was amazing how much emotion was still attached to these incidents so many years later.

I remembered being promised by my friend's aunt to be driven up to a lake cabin where my friend was spending a couple weeks in the summer. The aunt cancelled going the day before we were supposed to leave; I was crushed.

Broken Promises are Remembered

One 50-year-old woman recalled being afraid of going down the slide at a pool. Her dad was in the water and promised her that he would catch her. However, when she came sliding down, he didn't catch her.

She popped right up after being under water and reasoned that her dad probably just wanted her to learn that she could do it. However, she still resented the fact that he said he would catch her and he didn't. She clearly remembers that broken promise and her feelings of being deceived.

Strong Feelings from Broken Promises

How do we feel when promises are broken? We often feel betrayed and let down.

A broken promise affects our ability to trust that person in the future. Given the significance of promises, it is really important that we only make promises to our children that we are confident we can keep.

Only make promises you are sure you can keep.

Chapter 3: Responding Positively to Misbehavior

When we respond to our children's misbehavior in a new way, we usually get different results. This chapter guides you through focusing on one problem at a time and trying new ways of handling it.

Choosing New Approaches

Now that we've covered parenting behaviors to avoid, let's talk about what we can be doing instead. This chapter presents various parenting ideas to try.

Parents frequently state that what works well with child does not work for another child. This is so true! Since each of our children are different, we will need to figure out what works best with each child.

We all make mistakes – even parents! It's how we learn.

Being Patient with Yourself

Parenting is really difficult. Our children challenge us and cause us to grow in ways we never imagined before having kids. Any parent reading this book deserves a lot of credit for working hard to be the best parent possible.

Try to not be too hard on yourself if you don't handle a parenting situation ideally. Instead, dedicate yourself to figuring out a better approach for next time.

One mom said she was so happy to hear in one of the Priceless Parenting lessons that it took me a couple years of practice before I was able to primarily respond with empathy rather than anger to my children's misbehavior. She was pleased to know she didn't have to accomplish this in just a couple weeks! Changing your own behavior takes time, dedication and plenty of practice.

Taking parenting classes or reading parenting books should increase your skills while leaving you feeling better about your parenting, not worse. While there isn't one parenting technique that will magically work with all children, there are many approaches that work extremely well.

Focusing On One Problem at a Time

Parents are generally most successful when they focus on one problem behavior at a time per child. On the next page you will find the Challenging Behavior Worksheet. This worksheet guides you through tracking one problem behavior at a time.

You can make copies of this worksheet or use a notebook to record this information. If you would like to print out extra copies from your computer, you can find this document online at

http://www.PricelessParenting.com/documents/cbw.pdf

Use the ideas in the rest of this chapter to figure out new approaches in responding to these challenging behaviors.

Challenging Behavior Worksheet

What is one of your children's behaviors that you currently find difficult?

_____

_____

_____

How do you typically respond to this behavior?

_____

_____

_____

What new response will you try?

_____

_____

_____

What was the result of using this new response?

_____

_____

_____

Asking Your Child for Ideas

Your children may have some very good ideas about why they are choosing to behave in ways that you find challenging. If they are old enough, you can begin by asking them for their thoughts on this. After you understand their motivations, explain your concerns with the behavior.

Finally ask your child for ideas on how to satisfy both his needs and yours. You might just be surprised at what he says!

Helping Tweens and Teens Think Through Their Behavior

Once children are tweens or teens, many parents ground their children as a consequence for misbehavior. The hope is that by requiring teens to stay at home and not be with friends, teens will learn to make better choices. However, teens are probably more likely to spend their time thinking about how to not get caught in the future!

An approach which is more likely to encourage teens to learn from a poor choice is to ask them to write about it. One dad explained how he used this technique with his son, Tim.

Tim had gone to the movie theater with friends but when they got there the movie was sold out so they decided to walk to a nearby park and hang out instead. The dad was upset because Tim failed to update him and he was worried when Tim didn't come home after the movie.

Instead of grounding him, the dad asked Tim to write about the situation answering questions like:

- What was the sequence of events that happened?

- What influenced your actions?

- What would you do differently next time?

- What type of amends do you think you should make for this situation?

The dad explained that he would decide on any further consequences based on Tim's reflection.

Struggling to write down the answers to these types of tough questions can help teens learn from their poor choices. While they may be tempted to blame others for their actions, the goal of this exercise is for them to realize their own role in the situation and take responsibility for the results of their actions.

How could responding with empathy help you better handle your child's challenging behavior?

Allowing Children to Solve Their Own Problems

When we allow children to solve their own problems, we help them realize how capable and creative they are. They also learn to figure out how to handle difficult situations by themselves.

Whose problem is it?

Christine Hohlbaum, author of the book <u>S.A.H.M. I Am: Tales of a Stay-at-Home Mom in Europe</u>, wrote about her success in allowing her children to solve their own problems. After completing a lesson in the online Priceless Parenting class, she described how the new ideas worked:

When children are bored, it's their problem not yours!

'Fresh off Lesson #3 from today's parenting course, I jumped into it with vigor.

"I'm bored!" my son whined.

"Oh, what are you going to do?" I asked.

He was stunned.

Normally, I offer helpful hints, tips and tricks to avoid the Boredom Monster. After he recovered from his initial shock, my son said, "I think I'll call Anton." He quickly got distracted with something his sister was doing, then proudly announced 30 minutes later that he decided now would be a good time to call his friend. They made a playdate. After a quick peck on the cheek, he was out the door.

My daughter, who tends to challenge me wherever I go, looked me squarely in the eye and said, "I'm doing the rest of my homework after dance class." She laid out a sensible plan. "Sounds like you know what you are doing!" was all I said. Another stunned silence ensued. No bickering? Commanding? Bossing around? I smiled sweetly and wished her good luck. My daughter looked about her, put on her shoes, and left for Hip Hop.

Fast-forward a few hours. The kids came home. My daughter dilly-dallied. It started to get late.

"Oh, didn't you say you were going to read outloud?" She claimed she already had. When I reminded her she had said she would do so in front of her father, she had no where to go. "Are you going to read now or after your shower?" She started to squirm. I could tell my calm, question-based parenting was started to sink in. It really is her responsibility to make certain things get done in her life.'[1]

Could allowing your children to solve their own problems help with their challenging behaviors?

Using Short Responses

When we respond to our children's misbehavior using lots of words, we are giving them a lot of attention. This may be negative attention but any attention will encourage a behavior to continue. So our goal is to limit the words we use when our children are misbehaving.

For example, one dad described a situation where his daughter was begging him to buy a stuffed bear at the store. He had already told her he wouldn't buy it for her and then she started in with *"oh p-l-l-le-e-e-e-a-s-s-e Daddy, I'll be really good the rest of the day if I can just have it."* Instead of launching into an explanation of why he wasn't buying it, he just responded *"I know you're disappointed. What was my answer?"*[2]

Lots of Words = Lots of Attention

Short responses to behaviors like whining and begging will help extinguish those behaviors. The more attention we pay to a behavior, the more likely we are to see that behavior. Be careful what you reinforce!

Powerful 1 - 2 Word Reminders

I saw two young boys goofing around in a grocery store parking lot, not paying attention to the traffic around them. Their dad said *"parking lot"*. That's all he said. The boys quickly stopped messing around and paid attention to where they were.

One or two word reminders can be effective while saving you from accidentally launching into a mini-lecture *("How many times do I have to remind you to be careful in parking lots!? There are cars ...")*.

Some short reminders parents have used include:

- *"Coat"* (remember to take your coat along)

- *"Shoes"* (it's time to put your shoes on so we can go)

- *"Towel"* (your wet towel needs to be hung up)

A mom told me that when her daughter forgot to put her dirty dishes in the dishwasher after dinner she would just say *"plate"* and walk away. She said using a one word reminder was effective and prevented her from ranting at her daughter.

Could a short response be useful in dealing with your child's challenging behavior?

Saying What You Will Do Instead Of What They Have To Do

When we tell children what they have to do, we are setting ourselves up for a power struggle. Ultimately, our children do not have to do what we order them to do.

In her book, Positive Discipline, Jane Nelson discusses that is often "better to decide what you will do than to try to make a child do something."[3] When you say what you are going to do, you can certainly make that happened!

Orders: Telling Them What To Do   **Statements: Saying What I Will Do**

Orders: Telling Them What To Do	Statements: Saying What I Will Do
"Don't look at me that way!"	"I'll be happy to speak to you when you are looking at me in a respectful way."
"Stop your whining!"	"I'll be happy to listen to you when your voice sounds like mine."
"Pick up your toys."	"You can pick up your toys or I'll pick them up and put them in the Earn Back Box."
"Quit fighting!"	"Your fighting is bothering me so I'm going outside to do some gardening."
"Put your dirty clothes in the laundry basket."	"I'll wash whatever clothes are in the laundry basket."
"Get your shoes on!"	"I'll be waiting for you in the car."

Taking Action Instead of Giving Orders

One mom described her frustration when her son would start splashing water out of the bathtub. Telling him to stop splashing wasn't working. She finally solved the problem by gently taking him out of the tub and drying him off whenever he started splashing water.

She didn't get angry but instead calmly told him that bath time was over. She reported that he quickly learned to not splash in the tub so he could enjoy more time playing in the water.

Does your child's challenging behavior involve not obeying your orders? How could you replace your orders with telling them what you are going to do?

Asking Once

Have you ever heard parents say to their child *"How many times do I need to ask you?"* When we ask children repeatedly to do something, we train them to expect multiple requests before they need to take any action.

Expect Action After First Request

Sometimes we unintentionally teach our children not to respond the first time we make a request. If children have learned that they really don't need to pay attention to us until we're screaming, then they often will wait until this point to respond. However, if we instead ask only once and expect it be done, children are more likely to act on our initial request.

Teach your children to respond on your first request.

For example, suppose you asked your child to pick up the jacket he just tossed on the floor. If your child starts playing with a toy instead of picking up his jacket, one way to guide him is to touch him gently on the shoulders and say *"I need you to hang up your jacket now."* This will help get his attention while letting him know that you expect him to do what you've asked.

You could also state your expectation saying *"Feel free to play with that toy just as soon as your jacket is hung up."* What will you do if your child still doesn't pick up his jacket? There are many possibilities including taking away the toy until the jacket is picked up. By taking action instead of simply repeating the request, you are teaching your child to respond the first time you ask.

Listening the First Time

When we teach our children to listen the first time, we are giving them responsibility for remembering and acting. On the other hand, continually reminding children puts the responsibility back on us.

Suppose our child's library book is due at school tomorrow and we've asked him to put it in his backpack. At this point, it's up to him to take action.

If he forgets, he won't be able to check another book out of the library. As long as we can stop ourselves from reminding him again, he will learn from the consequences.

If your child's challenging behavior involves not listening the first time, what could you do differently when this happens?

Turning a "No" into a "Yes"

People respond better to hearing "*yes*" to their requests rather than hearing "*no*". When you can turn a "*no*" into a "*yes*", you can grant your children's requests on your terms.[4]

You can do this by stating the circumstances under which the request will be granted. Below are some examples of saying both no and yes to a request.

"Can I have a cookie?"

- *"No, it's almost dinner time."*

- *"Yes, after dinner you can have a cookie."*

"Can we get a dog?"

- *"No, we're not getting a dog."*

- *"Yes, when you move out and have your own house, you can have a dog."*

"Can I go over to Sam's house?"

- *"No, you need to get your homework done."*

- *"Yes, feel free to go to Sam's house just as soon as your homework is done."*

"Can I watch a movie?"

- *"No, it's a school night."*

- *"Yes, on Friday night you can watch a movie."*

"Can I have $5?"

- *"No, you've already been given your allowance for the week."*

- *"Yes, I'd be happy to give you $5 if you mow the yard."*

Finding a way to say "yes" will produce more positive results.

How could responding with a conditional "yes" rather than "no" affect your child's challenging behavior?

Setting Effective Limits

Parents need to set limits whenever their child's behavior is causing a problem for themselves or someone else. An effective limit causes a decrease in the problem behavior over time.

Observing When Limits are not Effective

Many young children will try hitting their parents. One mom described how her daughter started hitting her when she was about 9-months-old.

Mom was very surprised and responded by calmly saying *"no hitting, nice"* and rubbing the girl's hand gently on her face. However, she continued hitting and Mom resorted to sternly grabbing her hands and saying *"No hit"*. This also didn't change her behavior.

Expect children to test limits.

By 18-months-old, she was hitting, scratching and pulling hair too! She did this with her mom, her dad and other kids. When she hit mom now, she immediately said *"nice"* and rubbed her hand on her mom's face. She's learned something but not what her mom had intended!

When parents respond to misbehavior in a way that doesn't effectively set a limit, children's misbehavior usually not only continues but escalates in an attempt to find the limit. In this case, the consequence of hearing *"no hitting"* and rubbing her mom's face did not discourage the girl from hitting. Instead, it actually encouraged her to try other behaviors to find the limit.

Setting Limits by Taking Action

Another mom knew she needed to allow less video game time when her 7-year-old son started not wanting to play outside or do things with the family preferring his video game instead. He was so attached to playing his video game that he often pitched a fit when he was told the game had to go off. His games didn't have a good way to save the game for later so he was reluctant to stop playing and lose his place in the game.

She decided to reduce his video game playing to one hour twice a week. She started giving him a 10 minute warning before his hour was up.

When the 10 minutes were up, he could either choose to shut the game off or she would turn the power off. It only took a couple times of turning the power off to get him to shut the game down in time.

Is your child's challenging behavior escalating? How could you set a more effective limit?

Identifying Underlying Feelings

Children need help in learning to identify and process their feelings. We can begin teaching children to recognize and express their feelings when they are young. By learning the words for different feelings, children develop their emotional vocabulary

Showing Empathy by Identifying with Feelings

Children feel more understood when we pay attention to their feelings. In <u>Raising an Emotionally Intelligent Child</u>, John Gottman describes five steps for emotionally coaching children and expressing empathy:[5]

1. Become aware of the child's emotions
2. Recognize the emotion as an opportunity for intimacy and teaching
3. Listen empathetically, validating the child's feelings
4. Help the child find words to label the emotion he is having
5. Set limits while exploring strategies to solve the problem at hand.

Show empathy by identifying with your child's feelings.

One mom used this process when her 4-year-old daughter got upset when challenged by something like trying to tie her shoes. However, she responded really well if her mom said *"You look really frustrated"*. Her daughter would launch into an explanation of how she was feeling very frustrated. She would also start calming down.

Covering Up Feelings with "I don't care"

During a parenting presentation, one parent asked *"What can I do when my child brings home a test where he did poorly and when I ask him about it he says 'I don't care.'?"*

The principal at this school gave some wise advice. She said that whenever she hears a student say *"I don't care"*, she tries to find the feelings and kernel of truth behind those words. She'll ask the child *"Can you tell me more about that?"* The real truth may be:

- I'm confused; I don't know how to do this.

- I need help but I don't know how to ask for it.

- I'm embarrassed because I don't understand this.

- I feel frustrated because I think this is too hard for me.

Once she understands what the child is really communicating, she is in a better position to help. Using empathy and careful listening can help uncover what is really going on.

How is your child feeling when doing this challenging behavior? If you're not sure, ask your child.

Standing Firm without Arguing

Once you've given your children an answer to a request, using simple responses can help you avoid being pulled into an argument. It can also leave you feeling calmer because you aren't feeling forced to come up with new explanations and reasons for your decision.

Anthony Wolf talks about this idea in his book, <u>The Secret of Parenting</u>, "Perhaps the toughest rule with decision making is that once you decide, you must stand firm. It is a disaster for all when children can regularly wear down their parents and get them to change their minds." He discusses using simple responses to stand firm.[6]

Once you've made a decision, stick to it without arguing.

Examples of Simple Responses

Simple phrases or questions work best in response to pleading. For example, if your child wants to play more video games after you've said the time is up and he starts begging you to play longer, you might say:

- *"What was my answer?"* or
- *"I hear you are disappointed."*

Every time he asks you again, you simply repeat the response. If he says something like *"That's not fair!"* you can respond:

- *"Probably not."* or
- *"I understand you're not happy with stopping."*

It's easier to stay calm when you repsond the same way every time he comes up with another reason why he should be allowed to have more time to play video games.[7]

Avoiding Argments

If he tries to engage you in arguing by saying *"Everyone else in my class gets to play video games for at least an hour a day.",* you can respond:

- *"Regardless ..."*
- *"I understand you're upset."*

Avoid defending your position with something like *"I don't believe that everyone else in your class even has video games let alone gets to play them an hour each day."*

By not engaging in a discussion around his objections, you avoid being pulled into an argument.

Could standing firm using a simple response be helpful in dealing with your child's challenging behavior?

Waiting for Compliance

Sometimes the best option when children do not immediately comply with a request is to repeat the request in a matter-of-fact manner and wait. After repeating your request, do not respond to anything further that they do or say until they have done what you asked.

Patiently Waiting

In The Secret of Parenting, Anthony Wolf, describes a situation where a dad has asked his son to quit banging his fork on the table but his son didn't stop. Here's the response he recommends:

Patience is a virtue!

"Your basic stance as you wait for them to comply should be the same as your attitude while waiting for a bus:

- I am here.
- I am waiting.
- I expect you to stop.
- I am not enjoying the wait.
- I am not going anywhere until you do what I have asked."

Most kids will comply when you take this approach at which point you can say "thank you".[8]

Learning to Comply with Rules

One of essential skills any preschooler needs to develop is the ability to follow directions. Parents play a critical role in teaching this skill to their children. One preschool teacher told me that all but one of their 70 preschool children had managed to learn to follow directions during the first four months of school. The one child, Jake, who refused to follow directions caused a huge disruption to the rest of the class.

For example, one of the school rules is that all children must put on their jackets before they go out to play. The kids can take off their jackets and hang them up outside if they are too warm, however, they need to put them on before they go outside.

Jake frequently refused to put on his jacket. When the teachers discussed the issue with Jake's parents, his dad replied that Jake doesn't like wearing a jacket and they don't make Jake do things he doesn't want to do.

While it may be easier in the short run to not insist that Jake comply with the rules, in the long run Jake's parents are failing to teach him important social skills.

If you wait patiently, will your child comply with your request to stop his challenging behavior?

Teaching Children to Use "I Statements"

Children need to learn how to use words rather than physical force to let someone else know what they want. One way is to teach children to use an "I statement".

The Format of "I Statements"

There are four parts to an "I Statement":

I feel _____ (mad, sad, glad, lonely, scared, …)

when you _____

because _____

and I want _____.

Starting a statement with "I" instead of "You" is assertive and less likely to make the listener defensive.

Practicing "I Statements"

When children are fighting over something, it is a perfect time for them to use an "I statement".

For example, four-year-old Madison was upset because her five-year-old sister Samantha wouldn't share the paint with her. Madison was about to hit Samantha when her mom decided to intervene and help her learn to use words to let Samantha know how she felt.

Both girls stopped painting while their mom walked them through using "I statements". Madison told her sister *"I feel mad when you won't share the red paint with me because I need red for my flower and I want you to share it with me."*

Next Samantha repeated back what Madison said (to insure the message was heard). Once she got it correct, it was Samantha's turn for an "I statement." Her statement was *"I feel rushed when you keep asking for the red paint because I'm not done with it yet and I want to finish using it."*

Madison then repeated back what she heard. Mom then left it up to Madison and Samantha to figure out if they could find a way to share the red paint or if mom needed to put the paint away.

Try creating an "I Statement" about your child's challenging behavior. If it makes sense, tell your child your "I Statement" and then listen carefully to his "I Statement".

Telling Children What They Can Do

It's easy to get into the habit of telling our children what we don't want them to do instead of what we want them to do. When reading *"Don't think of a red fire truck."* most people will automatically picture a red fire truck. When we want our children to change their behavior, we increase the likelihood of success by telling them what to do instead of what not to do.

Describing the behavior we do not want:

- *"Don't run!"*
- *"Stop yelling."*
- *"Don't give me that look!"*
- *"No throwing cars!"*

Make requests without using "no", "don't", "stop"

It's better to say what we do want:

- *"Please walk."*
- *"Please use your soft voice."*
- *"I'll be happy to talk to you when you are looking at me in a respectful way."*
- *"You can push the cars on the track."*

Applying it to the Skill of Sharing

While teaching children to share isn't easy, it can help to discuss our expectations for sharing ahead of time.

For example, before other children come over to play we may want to talk to our children about sharing and allow our children to select one special toy that can be put away which does not need to be shared. When their friends come over to play, all other toys need to be shared.

These are the behaviors we've told our children we want:

- Select one toy to be put away and not shared.
- Share all other toys with friends.

Even after discussing sharing in advance, it is likely for young playmates to get in a fight over a toy. We can then help them figure out how they might be able to share the toy. We will be teaching them an essential friendship skill!

Would telling your child what she can do, instead of what she can't do, reduce her challenging behavior?

Shaping the Desired Behaviors

Parents shape their children's behavior by what they pay attention to. By noticing good behavior, we increase the likelihood of seeing more of that behavior. It is more effective to focus on what we want them to do instead of what we don't want them to do.

Shaping Behavior

Dr. Kazdin, a psychologist who has helped many families, has carefully studied and applied research on shaping children's behavior. He's seen great success in using programs where kids collect points for doing certain behaviors and then turn those points in for rewards. He's captured this process in his book The Kazdin Method for Parenting the Defiant Child.[9]

Reward the desired behavior to see more of it.

The method begins with parents thinking of the positive opposite of whatever behavior they want to stop. For example, if a child throws tantrums whenever it's time to go to bed, then the positive opposite would be getting ready for bed, going to bed and staying there without screaming or hitting. Kazdin describes how to set up a reward system that encourages children in moving towards this new behavior.

One key component is that children are rewarded for small steps in the right direction. Parents are taught to give enthusiastic praise and points whenever a child performs a portion of the new behavior. The child can then earn rewards with the points.

The rewards range from small ones like choosing what book to read at bedtime to earning a trip to the zoo. The reward program usually lasts only a few weeks until the child masters the new behavior.

Providing Practice Using Role Plays

Practicing appropriate behavior is another effective way for children to learn the behavior that is expected. For example, if your children are continually interrupting you when you are on the phone, practicing how to behave using a role play might help.

Sometime when you're not busy, you could have the children sit down while you pretend to be talking on the phone. Their job is to not interrupt you for a couple minutes. If they do interrupt you, then you can start the timer over.

When you consider your child's challenging behavior,
what is the positive opposite behavior that you do want?
How can you encourage small steps in the right direction?

Allowing Natural Consequences to Teach

The older children become the more natural consequences tend to shape their behavior. The most difficult part for most parents is not interfering with natural consequences by rescuing their children.

When our children are experiencing natural consequences, it is always good to show genuine compassion. It is important to avoid saying things like *"Didn't I tell you this would happen?"*.

Natural consequences work well if we allow them to.

Suffering natural consequences

Beatrix Potter's classic story, "The Tale of Peter Rabbit", demonstrates letting natural consequences teach:

- Peter's mom was wise. She warned Peter not to go into Mr. McGregor's garden. When he went anyway, he got into plenty of trouble with Mr. McGregor just as she had told him might happen.

- Like many children, although Peter had been warned, he still needed to learn from his own mistakes. Mom went on with her own tasks and did not try to prevent Peter from making a mistake nor did she rescue him.

- Peter suffered many natural consequences like losing his shoes and jacket, becoming lost and scared, getting sick and missing out on a good dinner. Peter's mom avoided giving him a lecture while letting him experience the consequences.

Peter's mom allowed him to learn a lot that day!

Pointing Out Possible Natural Consequences

A mom told a story about her 15-year-old daughter announcing one evening that she had decided she was going to start smoking. Although the mom strongly felt this was not a good idea, she resisted the urge to share her viewpoint. Instead she replied, *"I hope smoking doesn't interfere with your singing."*

The next morning when her daughter came down for breakfast she declared that she had decided against smoking because she really wanted to have the best singing voice possible. Her mom was thrilled that she had changed her mind! She was also happy she held herself back from giving her daughter a lecture about the evils of smoking.

What is the natural consequence of your child's challenging behavior?

Deciding on Appropriate Consequences

The goal of discipline is to help children learn from their mistakes. The goal is not to serve as retribution to make them pay for the mistake.

Sometimes when children do something inappropriate there are no natural consequences. In these situations a logical consequence may be appropriate.

Choosing Logical Consequences

In her book <u>Kids Are Worth It</u>, Barbara Coloroso explains that consequences should ideally be:[10]

Discipline: comes from Latin disciplina meaning teaching or learning

- Reasonable: The consequence relates to the behavior and is not too severe.

- Simple: The consequence is obvious and can be delivered easily and quickly.

- Valuable: The consequence allows the child to learn from the mistake and make amends.

- Practical: The consequence is achievable and makes sense given the child's age and behavior.

Some things to conside include:

- What can my child do to help make amends for the mistake?

- How can a consequence help my child make better choices in the future?

- How can I use empathy so my child is in a thinking state and maintains his self-esteem?

Children can be asked what they think is a reasonable consequence. Getting their buy-in makes the consequence much more likely to have a positive outcome.

Showing Our Disappointment

Sometimes expressing our disappointment is all the consequence that is needed. For example, if our child takes a piece of cake without asking, we may only need to say *"I'm very disappointed that you took that brownie without asking because I was planning to bring it to the school meeting."*

Does some type of consequence make sense in response to your child's challenging behavior?

Taking "Cool Down" Time

Taking time to cool down can be helpful for children and parents alike! Having a break allows people to regroup and regain their composure. After emotions have cooled, everyone is in a better place for thinking about the situation.

Time-Outs Remove Attention

When a child leaves the situation for a time-out, he is no longer getting attention. Since behavior that gets attention is likely to be repeated, removing the attention helps.

Time-outs provide breathing room.

Key Points for Making Time-Outs Work

According to the Pediatric Development and Behavior's article "What Makes Time-Out Work (and Fail)?" make sure these items are in place for time-outs to be effective:[11]

- Provide a rich, nurturing "time-in" environment so that the children want to be there.

- When you ask your child to take a time-out, make the request unemotionally, using few words. Do not give lots of warnings before implementing a time-out.

- Do not give children attention while they are in time-out.

- Focus on building self quieting skills versuis a time limit. Allow children to leave time-out once they have quieted themselves and feel they are ready to rejoin the group.

- Use other strategies to teach children new skills. If your child's behavioral problem is due to a lack of skills, teach the missing skills instead of sending him to time-out.

- Be consistent in how time-outs are given.

When your child comes back from time-out, be sure to be welcoming and avoid giving a lecture about why he was sent to time-out. Children are usually able to figure out why they were sent to time-out.

Would taking a time-out help reduce your child's challenging behavior?

Establishing Simple Rules

Simple, easy-to-remember rules work well with young children. One way to make sure children understand a rule is to ask them to explain the rule in their own words.

Crying means stop

One mom's rule for her 3-year-old and 18-month-old is *"Crying means stop."* Her kids have learned that if someone is crying then it's time to stop whatever they are doing.

Both children know the rule and are often able to stop themselves from whatever they are doing when someone starts crying. However, she does step in if the children are unable to stop themselves or the situation is escalating. By allowing her children to work out most of their problems on their own, she is giving them the opportunity to learn the important skill of self-control.

Simple rules work great for young children.

If you hit, you sit.

This is a simple rule which lets young children know the consequence of hitting. Parents can explain to children that they are welcome to stay if they choose to play cooperatively, *"We want to feel safe when we are together and so if you choose to hit, you must leave."*

If children hit:

- Guide them to sitting down nearby (this will probably motivate them to quickly change their behavior in order to rejoin the fun) or have them go to their room.

- Let children decide when they are ready to return. Tell them they are welcome to come back as soon as they decide to play without hitting.

- Stay calm and avoid showing anger or disappointment. By keeping your emotions under control, children can focus on their own behavior.

- Welcome children back, *"I'm happy you've decided to come back. It's more fun when you're with us."*

Eventually children will develop self-control. Until that time, parents need to intervene when their children are hitting.

Is there a simple rule that could help with your child's challenging behavior?

Conclusion

I much prefer the saying "practice makes better" to "practice makes perfect" especially when it comes to parenting. There are no perfect parents and trying to achieve some type of perfection often leads to feeling inadequate as a parent. However, we can all improve our parenting through practicing.

Ideally we want to parent in a way that helps our children develop good moral characteristics like honesty, responsibility, self-reliance, kindness, cooperation and self-control. As most parents will readily admit, this is much easier said than done!

How exactly do we parent in a way that brings these characteristics out in our children? Hopefully you've gotten some helpful ideas from this book. I'd love to hear your parenting stories. Please send them to me at Kathy.Slattengren@PricelessParenting.com

I wish you all the best in your parenting and leave you with these words:

"I have come to the frightening conclusion that I am the decisive element. It is my personal approach that creates the climate. It is my daily mood that makes the weather.

I possess tremendous power to make a life miserable or joyous. I can be a tool of torture or an instrument of inspiration. I can humiliate or humor, hurt or heal.

In all situations, it is my response that decides whether a crisis will be escalated or de-escalated and a person humanized or dehumanized.

If we treat people as they are, we make them worse. If we treat people as they ought to be, we help them become what they are capable of becoming."

- Johann Wolfgang von Goethe

About The Author

Kathy Slattengren is an internationally recognized parenting educator and founder of Priceless Parenting. She is dedicated to teaching parents critical skills needed for effectively responding to their children's behavior while building warm, loving relationships.

While raising her own two children, she learned many wonderful parenting techniques from classes, seminars and books. Through studying research, she discovered a universal body of knowledge about how effective parents do their job.

Her Masters of Education degree from the University of Washington combined with her Bachelor's degree in Psychology and Computer Science from the University of Minnesota enabled her to pull together parenting research into classes that are easy to understand and apply.

Parents report how much happier and calmer their homes are after applying ideas from Priceless Parenting. The online parenting classes allow parents to learn these valuable skills at their own pace and from the comfort of their own home.

Kathy and her husband have been married over 20 years and live in Seattle with their two teenagers.

You can keep up with Priceless Parenting ideas by signing up for the free monthly newsletter. Each month focuses on a common parenting challenge incorporating stories from real parents along with suggestions for applying the information to your own family. Sign up at **http://www.PricelessParenting.com**.

You can join in the conversation by participating in Priceless Parenting's Facebook page:

http://www.facebook.com/PricelessParenting

References and Notes

Chapter 1: Guiding and Encouraging Children

[1] Nelsen, Jane. Positive Discipline. New York, NY: Ballantine Books, 2006, p. 247.

[2] Ford, Judy. Wonderful Ways to Love a Child. Boston, MA: Red Wheel/Wiser, 2003, p.38.

[3] Bailey, Becky. Easy to Love, Difficult to Discipline. New York, NY: HarperCollins Publisher, 2000, p.206.

[4] Perry, Bruce and Szalavitz Maia. Born for Love: Why Empathy is Essential and Endangered. New York, NY: HarperCollins Publisher, 2010, p.12.

[5] Pink, Daniel. Drive: The Surprising Truth About What Motivates Us. Riverhead Hardcover, 2009.

[6] Jacobs, Tom. "The Two Faces of Perfection". Miller-McCune (2010). URL: http://www.miller-mccune.com/culture-society/the-two-faces-of-perfectionism-8137/

[7] Cash, Hilarie and McDaniel, Kim. Video Games & Your Kids. Enumclaw, WA: Idyll Arbor, 2008, p. 84.

Chapter 2: Parenting Behaviors to Avoid

[1] Bradley, Michael. Yes, Your Teen is Crazy. Gig Harbor, WA: Harbor Press, 2003, p.180.

[2] Nelsen, Jane. Positive Discipline. New York, NY: Random House, 2006, p.198.

Chapter 3: Responding Positively to Misbehavior

[1] Hohlbaum, Christine. S.A.H.M. I Am: Tales of a Stay-at-Home Mom in Europe. Wyatt-MacKenzie Publishing, 2005.

[2] Fay, Jim and Cline, Foster. Becoming a Love and Logic Parent course handout "Two Ways to Neutralize Childhood Arguing" teaches that most "one-liners" or simple responses are designed to avoid the "hook" and not to argue with the ridiculous, 1993.

[3] Nelsen, Jane. Positive Discipline. New York, NY: Random House, 2006, p.19.

[4] Faber, Adele and Mazlish, Elaine. How to Talk So Kids Will Listen & Listen So Kids Will Talk, 1980, p. 161. They discuss substituting a "yes" for a "no" whenever possible.

[5] Gottman, John, Declaire, Joan and Goleman, Daniel. Raising an Emotionally Intelligent Child. New York, NY: Fireside, 1997, p. 76-80.

[6] Wolf, Anthony. <u>The Secret of Parenting: How to Be in Charge of Today's Kids--from Toddlers to Preteens--Without Threats or Punishment</u>. New York, NY: Farrar, Straus and Giroux, 2000.

[7] Fay, Jim. <u>An Introduction to Love and Logic: How to Discipline Kids without Losing their Love and Respect</u>, 2004, p. 65, "Rather than letting the arguing get to you, go 'brain dead' by calmly repeating a phrase over and over, regardless of what your child says."

[8] Wolf, Anthony. <u>The Secret of Parenting: How to Be in Charge of Today's Kids--from Toddlers to Preteens--Without Threats or Punishment</u>. New York, NY: Farrar, Straus and Giroux, 2000.

[9] Kazdin, Alan. <u>The Kazdin Method for Parenting the Defiant Child</u>. New York, NY: Houghton Mifflin Harcourt Publishing Company, 2009.

[10] Coloroso, Barbara. <u>Kids Are Worth It! : Giving Your Child The Gift Of Inner Discipline</u>. New York, NY: HarperCollins Publisher, 2002, p. 84-85.

[11] Pediatric Development and Behavior, "What Makes Time-Out Work (and Fail)?", 6/11/2007.

Made in the USA
Charleston, SC
22 December 2010